How to Write a Composition

Grades 6-10

Written by T.R. Gadd, B.A., M.Ed.

ISBN 1-55035-534-1
Copyright 1997
Revised January 2006

Published in the United States by:
On the Mark Press
3909 Witmer Road PMB 175
Niagara Falls, New York
14305
www.onthemarkpress.com

Published in Canada by:
S&S Learning Materials
15 Dairy Avenue
Napanee, Ontario
K7R 1M4
www.sslearning.com

Look For Other Language Units

Table of Contents

This resource is designed as a companion piece to How to Write an Essay and How to Write a Paragraph. Its aim is to help students write various kinds of compositions from grades six through the first years of secondary school. It will be helpful for students at higher levels of education who have had difficulty with writing in earlier years.

The resource contains many work sheets which can be used individually by students or in groups. Many of these work sheets are most useful if completed by pairs of students. It is also advisable for students to discuss the ideas generated by the work sheets in larger groups.

Much of this resource is written from a students perspective, so that teachers may give students the pages which they need or so that students can purchase the resource to use as they write their compositions at home.

1. WHAT IS A COMPOSITION?

To compose is to make up, invent or put together something. A **composition**, then, is the thing composed. It can be a piece of writing or a piece of music, made up, invented or put together by the composer.

A composition usually refers to a series of connected paragraphs. Of course a single paragraph is *composed* by its writer, but normally the word composition means a longer piece of writing.

Each paragraph in the composition must possess two important qualities: **unity** and **coherence**.

Unity means that there is only one idea in each paragraph. This means that all the sentences in the paragraph will talk about only one main idea. Sentences which discuss other ideas will not be included in the paragraph. This main idea is included in the **topic sentence**. Usually the topic sentence is the first sentence in the paragraph, but it does not have to be. Sometimes the topic sentence is placed in the middle of the paragraph or at the end, but it is a good idea for writers to place the topic sentence first in the paragraph; that way the reader knows exactly what the paragraph will be about. The **concluding sentence** is not only the last sentence in the paragraph, but it has another job: it sums up the main idea of the paragraph. A writer who pays attention to both topic sentence and concluding sentence will ensure that the paragraph possesses unity.

But the sentences in the paragraph also have to be arranged in an order that makes some sense. This arrangement of sentences is called **coherence**. If a paragraph possesses coherence, then one sentence will lead logically to the next; the writer will not skip around from one idea to another.

Finally, a composition requires **emphasis**. This simply means that the important ideas in the composition are emphasized. Emphasis can be achieved by placing important ideas in the most important places in the composition--usually at the beginning or at the end or in both places.

As a well written single paragraph possesses the qualities of unity and coherence, so a series of connected paragraphs possesses these qualities also, both **within** each paragraph and **within** the entire piece of writing. This means that each paragraph will possess unity; each paragraph will be concerned with one idea. All of these ideas together make up one topic and the writer does not include ideas or paragraphs which are off topic. Each paragraph can be considered as a subsection of the overall topic. If each paragraph possesses unity and if each paragraph discusses one aspect of the topic, then the entire composition will also possess unity.

Similarly, coherence will be gained within the composition through the arrangement of the paragraphs and the connections between them.

There are several ways in which paragraphs may be arranged in a composition. Some of these are:
- chronological order
- physical order
- order of importance
- order of climax

These specific methods of arrangement are discussed in more detail in the resource, *How to Write a Paragraph*, SSR1-09.

If the writer thinks of a composition as a train, with each paragraph representing a car, then, just as the train needs a coupling to attach the cars, a composition needs something to connect the paragraphs. These connections are called transitions. Transition words and phrases are words which refer to earlier or later parts of the composition; by doing so, they provide connections between the paragraphs and create a smooth flow of ideas. They create coherence.

The chart on page 5 provides examples of transition words which can express various types of arrangement in a composition.

1. WHAT IS A COMPOSITION?

Chart: Examples of Transition Words and Phrases

TYPE OF ARRANGEMENT	EXAMPLES	
TIME	then later during now presently	next before afterwards meanwhile eventually
PHYSICAL ORDER	to the right above under in the distance straight ahead	to the left below beside
ORDER OF IMPORTANCE	more importantly to some degree to a lesser extent	
SIMILAR IDEAS	in addition also and in the same way	similarly likewise moreover
DIFFERENT IDEAS	on the other hand on the contrary however nevertheless yet	but otherwise still
CONCLUSION	therefore so for this reason	thus hence

These are only some of the many transition or connecting words available in English.

1. WHAT IS A COMPOSITION?

Three major types of compositions are dealt with in this resource:

- exposition
- narration
- description.

Each of these three types of writing has a different purpose, and therefore each one is planned and constructed differently.

TYPES OF COMPOSITIONS

TYPE OF COMPOSITION	DEFINITION	PURPOSE
EXPOSITION	a detailed explanation which involves facts or opinions	to explain or inform to convince or persuade
NARRATION	a story with a plot, setting and characters	to entertain to inform or teach a lesson
DESCRIPTION	a detailed picture of the characteristics of an object, person or place	to inform to entertain

The writer of a composition must decide what type of composition he or she is writing. This will depend on the topic chosen and the purpose of the assignment. Students should note that many pieces of writing involve characteristics of all three types: A short story, for example, may include explanation (that is, exposition) and description. Similarly, an exposition may develop part of its explanation by telling a story or may use description. However, for most assignments in school, students will not go wrong if they decide to use one of these types of compositions.

Before beginning to write, students should ask themselves:

- What is the purpose of the writing assignment?
- What type of composition will best achieve this purpose?

Often the question or assignment will make this decision for the student. The assignment may be, for example, to write a short story or to write an explanation.

1. WHAT IS A COMPOSITION?

EXERCISE 1 ON TYPES OF COMPOSITIONS

In the chart which follows, you are given a topic for a composition. You are to decide what type of composition--exposition, narration or description--you would write for each topic. Then jot down ideas you could use to write a composition on the particular topic. The type of composition you choose will determine the ideas you use; therefore, for some of these topics, you could write any of the three types of composition.

TOPIC	TYPE OF COMPOSITION	IDEAS
1. What I did last summer		
2. My best friend		
3. The Wright Brothers		

1. WHAT IS A COMPOSITION?

EXERCISE 2 ON TYPES OF COMPOSITIONS

In the chart which follows, you are given a topic for a composition. You are to decide what type of composition--exposition, narration or description--you would write for each topic. Then jot down ideas you could use to write a composition on the particular topic. The type of composition you choose will determine the ideas you use; therefore, for some of these topics, you could write any of the three types of composition.

TOPIC	TYPE OF COMPOSITION	IDEAS
1. Solids, Liquids and Gases		
2. A character in a novel, play or movie I have read or seen		
3. Why I like being a hockey player, or a baseball player or....		

1. WHAT IS A COMPOSITION?

EXERCISE 3 ON TYPES OF COMPOSITIONS

In the chart which follows, you are given a topic for a composition. You are to decide what ideas you could use to write each type of composition on this topic--exposition, narration or description. Write down ideas you could use in the space provided in the chart. You may limit the topic if you wish.

TOPIC: The Zoo (or The Circus or The Amusement Park)

EXPOSITION	NARRATION	DESCRIPTION

1. WHAT IS A COMPOSITION?

EXERCISE 4 ON TYPES OF COMPOSITIONS

In the chart which follows, you are given a topic for a composition. You are to decide what ideas you could use to write each type of composition on this topic--exposition, narration or description. Write down ideas you could use in the space provided in the chart. You may limit the topic if you wish.

TOPIC: My Family Background

EXPOSITION	NARRATION	DESCRIPTION

2. WRITING AN EXPOSITION

The purpose of an exposition is to explain. There are many kinds of expositions, such as the following:

- the persuasive essay or argument
- a feature article for a newspaper
- a business memo
- a research paper
- a newspaper editorial
- a report
- a letter

Outside of school, many people must write various kinds of expositions in both their jobs and their personal lives. Letters, memos, sometimes even recipes, e-mail and so on have become very necessary part of our lives. So it is important that students learn to write expositions.

There are many ways by which a writer may explain. A writer may explain by:

- giving reasons or causes (explaining *why* something occurs)
- comparing (showing how two or more things are the same)
- contrasting (showing how two or more things are different)
- defining (explaining what something means)
- providing facts or evidence
- showing how to do something

Sometimes it is very difficult to explain something. We have all listened to people give directions on how to get to a certain place. Some people can do this well, whereas others have a great difficulty explaining. The exercises which follow should help students to explain more effectively.

EXERCISE 1 ON EXPLANATION

To try your skills in explanation, write a brief exposition (one or more paragraphs) on the following topics. Use the techniques for explaining which is given after each topic.

1. Why does a zebra have stripes? (Give reasons.)
2. I am like my mother or my father. (Use comparison.)
3. How is a star different from a planet? (Use contrast.)
4. What is chlorophyll? (Define.)
5. Why is Celine Dion (or any other famous singer) very popular? (Provide facts or evidence.)
6. How to make a peanut butter sandwich. (List the steps in order.)
7. Why did Columbus sail to the New World? (Give reasons.)
8. How is American football different from Canadian football? (Use contrast.)
9. What is a terrarium? (Define.)

2. WRITING AN EXPOSITION

EXERCISE 2 ON EXPLANATION

What technique or techniques of explanation would you use if you were writing an exposition on each of the following topics? Write your answer in the space provided. In the column headed **Why** explain why you have chose each technique.

TOPIC	TECHNIQUE(S)	WHY
1. Is a harmonica different from a mouth organ?		
2. My favorite sports figure is...		
3. I would like to live in the city (or the country).		

2. WRITING AN EXPOSITION

NEWSPAPER REPORTS

Newspaper reporters use many of the techniques for explanation outlined here. In order to write a good article, reports often use what they call *the four w's and the h*. These are questions which they must answer in order to write an accurate report. These questions are:

- Who?
- When?
- Where?
- Why?
- How?

The reporter needs to know who are involved in the story, when the story occurred, where it occurred, why it happened and how it happened. If the reporter can find the answers to these questions, the story will be accurate, detailed and probably interesting.

EXERCISE ON NEWSPAPER REPORTING

Pretend you are a reporter for a newspaper. Find the answer to the five questions (who? when? where? why? how?) on one of the following stories. Then write the story.

1. An activity which has just occurred or will be occurring at your school, such as a sports game, a dramatic or musical event, or a school announcement.

2. A planned or current concert tour by your favorite singer or band.

3. A trip that you family has made or plans to make.

4. An interesting event from history or science, such as a discovery or an invention.

2. WRITING AN EXPOSITION

FACT OR OPINION

It is important for all human beings to be able to tell the difference between facts and opinions. Unfortunately, many people cannot do this, and these people often express their opinions as if they were facts.

A **fact** is something that is true, something that really happened. Often what we think happened and what did happen are not the same. That is because we notice or remember only certain things, and we may not notice or remember things that are important. In addition, when we talk or write about something that happened, we sometimes use our judgment and our feelings. This use of judgment and feelings is called an **opinion**.

Sometimes when people use their opinions as if they were facts, there is not a serious problem. We often hear people say, "I just saw a bad movie." A statement like this one is an opinion. Someone else might see the same movie and call it a "good movie"; this too would be an opinion. In most cases, expressing an opinion like this one will do no harm. But sometimes the expressions of opinions as if they were facts will do harm. Throughout history, there have been people who considered certain groups to be inferior to themselves and this has led to prejudice and poor treatment of others.

A good opinion is one which is based on facts. When you wake up ill in the morning your mother may express the opinion that you have the flu. Unless your mother has particular knowledge of medicine and health, her opinion may or may not be a valid one. A doctor with his knowledge may discover the following facts: your temperature is 102°; you are breathing more heavily than you usually do; your heart rate is faster than normal; you have nasal congestion; etc. Based on these facts, he may conclude that you have the flu. This conclusion, however, is still an opinion. His opinion may be the same as your mother's opinion, but because of the facts on which he has based it, it has more weight.

Not all opinions, therefore, are of equal value. Two people may hold the same opinion, but only one may know the facts. People sometimes say, "Everyone has a right to an opinion." Note that this statement is also an opinion, but is it a valid opinion? Does a person have a right to an opinion which is not based on fact (called an **unfounded opinion**) if that opinion will hurt other people? Is an unfounded opinion from a person who knows little or nothing about the subject of equal value to the opinion of an expert in that subject?

It is important for the writer of expositions (especially essays or arguments which are statements of opinion) to know the difference between opinions and facts, and to use facts to support opinions. There are several ways for a writer or speaker to avoid expressing unfounded opinions. Some of these are:

- Do enough research, learn enough, to have a basis for forming an opinion. Do not form an opinion based on little knowledge. Then use this knowledge to support the opinions that you present.

- Avoid using generalizations. Sentences beginning with "Everyone knows...", or "All the students in my class..." usually have not been researched. Often the writer or speaker is expressing his or her own opinion and trying to make it sound important by saying that this opinion is held by "everyone" or "all the students in my class".

- Do not say that something "is", if it only "may be". "This statement is true" is not the same as "this statement may be true." Similarly, "It may be beneficial" for people to do a certain thing or behave a certain way might be a more accurate way of expressing an idea than by saying, "It is beneficial..."

- Watch out for unfounded opinions expressed by other people, both in writing and in speaking.

Learning how to use both facts and opinions is helpful in writing or reading expositions. This helps us to read a newspaper more critically and to judge the opinions of others. It also helps us to write essays and reports (coming up in the next few pages).

2. WRITING AN EXPOSITION

EXERCISE 1 IN FACT AND OPINION

In small groups, decide if each of the following statements is a fact or an opinion. Provide reasons for your answer.

1. *Nirvana* is the greatest rock group of all time.
2. Everyone in the class knows that O.J. Simpson is not guilty of murdering his wife.
3. Everyone in the class believes that O.J. Simpson is not guilty of murdering his wife.
4. In his criminal trial, O.J. Simpson was found not guilty of murdering his wife.
5. The best movie I have ever seen is *Jurassic Park*.
6. Mark McGuire is the best player who ever played for the St. Louis Cardinals.
7. If parents spent more time with their children, the children would grow up to be happier human beings.
8. Light travels in straight lines.
9. Columbus discovered American in 1492.
10. Jamaican people love to laugh and you can often see their smiling faces and know that they have a good sense of humor.
11. Science is a harder subject than English.

EXERCISE 2 IN FACT AND OPINION

What follows is an editorial for a newspaper. It did not actually appear in any newspaper, but assume that it did. In small groups, decide what statements are fact and what are opinion. Provide reasons for your answer.

What is wrong with teenagers these days? They don't know how to behave. They don't know how to dress. They have no respect for their elders.

We hear these kinds of statements all the time. But over 2 000 years ago in ancient Greece, Aristotle said much the same thing. It seems as if every generation is bent on putting down teens.

But what about the good teenagers? There are many of them and they are rarely mentioned in the newspapers or on television. What about Boy Scouts whose apple sales help to teach people to care about other human beings? What about the young boy in London, who last week saved three cats and a dog from a burning barn? What about the Olympic hopefuls who spend their days in training to be the best they can be? What about all those kids who play soccer, and baseball, and hockey, and basketball, and too many sports to mention? What about all those teenagers who work at the fast food restaurants and gas stations who are always polite and always willing to go the extra mile to help a customer? What about all those young adults who sit in classrooms in this nation and try their best to learn so that their country and their own future will be secure?

Yes, it's easy to pick on teenagers if you want to make unfounded generalizations which have no relationship to the facts. It's easy to read about one bad apple and say that the whole basket is bad. But why? Those good apples make awfully good pies if you aren't prepared to throw them out.

2. WRITING AN EXPOSITION

ESSAYS AND REPORTS

Fact and opinion become very important when a student is writing an essay or a report. As the earlier sections of this resource have shown, opinions are only worthwhile if they are based on facts. But there are occasions for writing where opinion is not considered important.

An **essay** is essentially an argument; that is, it is a judgment, an opinion or a point of view. It is important that this point of view be based on facts, observation or evidence. To this extent, an essay is **subjective**; this means that it is the expression of a personal opinion. Because it is an opinion, it is **arguable**; this means that the opposite point of view is also arguable.

"Donovan Bailey is the 1996 Olympic Gold Medalist in the 100 meter dash" is not arguable; it is a fact. "Donovan Bailey is the fastest man in the world" is arguable; the argument can be supported by evidence such as Bailey's time in the 1996 Olympics 100 meters, but not every man in the world has been tested under similar conditions. So one could also argue that other people are faster runners than Donovan Bailey. Thus, people could argue that Michael Johnson is a faster runner by citing his time in the 200 meter race at the Atlanta Olympics.

A **report** simply states the facts. Usually a report tells of the findings of the writer's research, and therefore there is no need for any opinions to be expressed. Thus, a report tends to be **objective**; this means that it deals only with information which can be considered factual. Because this information is presented objectively, it is **not arguable**. Some reports, however, do call for recommendations based on the facts presented--and this part of any report is arguable and is therefore like an essay.

A report on Kenya (or any other country) might consider its population, land area and major population centers, its imports and exports, the topography of the country, or other factors. In this report, the writer researches the information and presents the information to the reader. It is not usually necessary for the writer to make any personal comments or judgments on the information presented.

2. WRITING AN EXPOSITION

ESSAYS AND REPORTS

An **ESSAY** means a **PERSUASIVE ESSAY** or **ARGUMENT**. Often students in school are asked to write a **REPORT**, that is, a summary of research findings without a specifically expressed argument.

Arguments and Reports differ in **PURPOSE** and in **ORGANIZATION**:

	ESSAY	REPORT
PURPOSE	• to be subjective: to argue a specific point of view • to provide evidence to support this point of view	• to be objective: to present findings from research • to provide examples from the research
ORGANIZATION	• statement of thesis: overall argument and supporting arguments • explanation of each argument in turn, followed by presentation of evidence and examples • conclusion	• statement of scope and purpose of the report • summary of findings citing examples and sources • conclusion and recommendations if required

Students or the teacher may find more information on essays and reports in the resource, *How to Write an Essay*, SSR1-08.

2. WRITING AN EXPOSITION

SAMPLES OF ESSAYS AND REPORT TOPICS

Students usually are not asked to write essays in elementary school, but may be asked to do so in secondary school. Often elementary students are asked to write reports. The chart which follows shows the different approaches to a topic required by essays and reports.

	ESSAY	REPORT
Topic 1: The Senate	• The Senate should be abolished. • The Senate performs a useful check on government	• The organization of the Senate, including the number of members, how they are appointed, what areas they represent, etc.
Topic 2: Erosion	• A particular planting technique is more helpful than another in preventing soil erosion. • Many economic disasters might have been averted if farmers had taken measures to control erosion	• The advantages and disadvantages of various methods to control erosion. • Areas of the earth where erosion poses particular problems to the way of life of the inhabitants

2. WRITING AN EXPOSITION

EXERCISE 1 ON ESSAYS AND REPORTS

What follows are some topics which may be suitable for writing essays or reports. In the spaces provided write some ideas which you might use for an essay and for a report.

TOPIC	ESSAY IDEAS (arguments)	REPORT IDEAS (facts)
1. Women in Sports		
2. My Family		
3. My Chosen Career		

3. WRITING A NARRATIVE

Narration is the art of story telling.

From the time when we were very young, old enough to listen, we have been told stories. "Once upon a time there was a little girl named..." began many of the stories we heard when we were children. And it has been this way for centuries.

As a matter of fact, the first stories were likely told when people lived in caves as soon as they learned to speak and communicate their ideas. The first stories were probably told by the cave mother and the cave father. In order to keep the children away from the fire in the cave, the mother likely told a story about someone who was burned by the fire; this story had a moral or lesson for the children to learn to stay away from the fire. The cave father, whose job was to hunt animals probably told the first "fish story"; if he came home from the hunt empty-handed, he might have told a story about the big one that got away. In time his story could become a legend of great exploits.

Students are often asked to write stories in school because they are so familiar with story-telling. It is amazing how many stories written by students are like the first cave stories--either a warning to pay attention to some lesson or a story of bravery and great deeds. As a matter of fact, most stories that have been written are of those two types, warnings and great deeds.

What follows are some ideas on how to write stories, the art of narration. Of course, this is only a brief summary of a great art form.

3. WRITING A NARRATIVE
THE ELEMENTS OF SHORT STORY WRITING

A short story contains four elements--qualities which make it a story. The four elements are:

- plot
- characterization
- setting
- theme.

1. **Plot**: A plot is a series of connected events which lead to a climax. A plot usually has five parts to it:

    1. introduction: This part introduces the characters and the setting and sets up the **status quo** or situation in the story.

    2. complication: An event occurs which **changes** the situation set up in the introduction.

    3. crisis: continuing events occur to build suspense and bring the situation to its high point.

    4. climax: The highest point of action, where tension and suspense are greatest, and when the conflict must be resolved.

    5. dénouement: Order is restored and a new **status quo** is established.

2. **Characterization**: Characterization does not only mean people in a story. The reader needs to learn something about them, so the writer must describe their personality and their appearance. The personality of characters is often revealed in three ways:

    - by what they say
    - by what they do
    - by what other characters say about them.

3. **Setting**: The setting is the time and the place where the action takes place. A writer usually describes the setting directly by saying where and when the action occurs. But the writer might also describe it indirectly by letting the characters refer to time or place as they speak. A good writer will likely not dwell too long on descriptions of setting; he or she will let the setting be revealed more indirectly during the course of the action.

4. **Theme**: The theme is the underlying idea of the story. It is not the events which occur; the events make up the plot. The theme is the reason **why** the writer is writing the story. It may be a story about love or family conflict or human emotions. And the theme will be revealed by what happens (the plot) and the characters.

The following two descriptions may help the student writer to see the difference between **theme** and **plot**:

- <u>Romeo and Juliet</u> is a story about love in a world set on revenge and hatred. (**Theme**)

- <u>Romeo and Juliet</u> is a story of two young people who fall in love, but are unable to find happiness, and so take their own lives. (**Plot**)

In the first statement, we learn the underlying idea of the story--what the story will be about and what the writer wants the reader to learn from the story. In the second statement, we learn some of the events that take place in the story.

3. WRITING A NARRATIVE

THE GUIDING PRINCIPLES OF SHORT STORY WRITING

Because a short story is short, a writer does not have the means to fully develop each of the four elements. In a novel (a long short story), the writer may provide complete information on characters and setting, may have several complicated plots, may interweave several themes. But a short story is not long enough to allow the writer to do all this.

The short story writer, therefore, uses two principles to restrict the length of the story. These are:

- principle of limitation
- principle of selection

1. Principle of Limitation

Because of lack of space (most short stories are under 10 pages in length), the author limits the development of the four elements. This means that there will be one simple plot, usually only one setting which is not described in great detail, few characters with little development of each character (perhaps one major character trait), and one dominant theme. Much is therefore left to the imagination of the reader.

Note that the writer of the short story still tries to give the reader some indication of character development and setting. The characters are usually not simply names with no personality; they do show strong personality traits. They are, however, generally two dimensional, rather than fully rounded human beings. Similarly, the setting **does** get some description; it is not merely a place name, but a **sense** of place and time. By employing the principle of limitation in a short story, the author does face a challenge. That challenge is to convey a great deal of information in a little space.

2. Principle of Selection

The author **selects** one of the four elements--plot, setting, characterization, theme--and develops this element in greater detail. All elements are present, but one receives the treatment more than the others.

3. WRITING A NARRATIVE

STORY WRITING BY STUDENTS

Of course, students in grade five will not likely be writing short stories using the principles and ideas on the previous few pages. By grade eight or grade nine, many students should be able to use the ideas expressed here to write a short story. In grade five, it would be important to mention terms like plot, character and setting. In the following years, students could be introduced to more of the details of these three elements. Theme is a more difficult concept for young students to grasp and is probably best left to grade eight or grade nine.

As the teacher works with story telling, it would be a good idea to introduce students to some short stories by the master writers, both classic and contemporary authors. Some suggestions follow:

- Edgar Allen Poe, "The Cask of Amontillado": The vocabulary of this story is somewhat difficult, so the story is perhaps best left to grade nine. A more appropriate story for grade eight students might be "The Tell-Tale Heart", one of the most scary of all the stories by Poe. "The Fall of the House of Usher" is mainly a description of setting, with little real action but a great deal of implied horror; it is not for all tastes.

- Shirley Jackson, "The Lottery": Again this is a story for older students, not because of its vocabulary (which is relatively easy), but because of its theme of ritual and human sacrifice.

- Sir Arthur Conan-Doyl, "Silver Blaze": Really any of the Sherlock Holmes stories do well in grades seven and eight. The plot and the development of the characters of Holmes and Watson should be stressed.

- Hans Christian Andersen and the Brothers Grimm: Their fairy tales are famous, but usually in some squeaky clean form. Actually, the original tales are quite gruesome and may not be suitable for all children, particularly the younger ones.

- There are many excellent short stories now coming into anthologies from Africa, the Caribbean, South America and Asia. Teachers should take a close look at these stories from fine writers who are as yet little known.

Reading short stories should engender discussion, not only about the plot of the story, but also about the way the story was written. In this way, young writers can begin to learn an art form.

3. WRITING A NARRATIVE

EXERCISE 1 ON EXPOSITION AND NARRATION

An exposition is an explanation. Like a short story, exposition may explain a series of events. However, narration involves plot, whereas exposition does not. Plot provides connections between these events.

The king died and then the queen died is exposition because it simply provides the events; it is only an explanation of what happened.

The king died and then the queen died of grief has the beginnings of plot: the events now have a connection, a relationship.

What follows are two listings of events. One is exposition; the other is narration. Decide which is exposition and which is narration. Point out the relationships between events in the narration by underlining words or phrases which show the connection between the events.

1. Charles Dickens had very little formal education for two reasons. First, his father was sent to debtors' prison. Secondly, Charles as the second oldest of eight children had to find work to support the family. Charles went to work in a blacking factory, labeling pots of a substance used to shine fireplace grates. Charles disliked his job and dreamed of another life.

    This writing is an example of _____ .

2. Charles Dickens might have had some education, but his early life did not allow it. One day, after his father's debts had become impossible to pay, the officers of the law came to the house and took the elder Mr. Dickens away to prison. Having no other course of action, Mrs. Dickens found work for her son, Charles, in a blacking factory. Charles hated his days there, but he went to work willingly, knowing that he had a responsibility to support his family. Although he disliked his job, Charles dreamed of a better life for himself and his family.

    This writing is an example of _____ .

3. WRITING A NARRATIVE

EXERCISE 2 ON EXPOSITION AND NARRATION

An exposition is an explanation. Like a short story, exposition may explain a series of events. However, narration involves plot, whereas exposition does not. Plot provides connections between these events.

The king died and then the queen died is exposition because it simply provides the events; it is only an explanation of what happened.

The king died and then the queen died of grief has the beginning of plot: the events now have a connection, a relationship.

In the space provided, rewrite each of the following groups of sentences providing a new thought which connects them in a logical way to create the beginnings of a plot:

1. Kathryn played basketball well. She won the gold medal.

    _____

    _____

2. Joshua bought a lottery ticket. He won $300.00.

    _____

    _____

3. I ate my breakfast in a hurry. I ran to the bus stop. I did not want to be the last person in line to buy the concert tickets.

    _____

    _____

3. WRITING A NARRATIVE

EXERCISE 3 ON EXPOSITION AND NARRATION

Following is a paragraph which **explains** some events in William Shakespeare's play, <u>Romeo</u> and Juliet. These events are written in sequence as an exposition. Rewrite the events to make a short story by providing the logical connections between them.

1. Romeo and Juliet were married secretly.
2. Romeo met his friends, Mercutio and Benvolio, in the market place.
3. Tybalt, Juliet's cousin, came to the market place.
4. Tybalt insulated Romeo and tried to start a fight.
5. Romeo refused to fight Tybalt.
6. Mercutio thought Romeo was a coward.
7. Mercutio decided to fight Tybalt.
8. Tybalt killed Mercutio.
9. Romeo became angry.
10. Romeo killed Tybalt.

Write your story in the space below:

_____
_____
_____
_____
_____
_____
_____
_____
_____
_____
_____
_____
_____
_____
_____
_____

3. WRITING A NARRATIVE

CREATING SUSPENSE IN A STORY

The writer of a short story tries to keep the reader's interest in several ways. One of these ways is to create **suspense**. Suspense is a feeling created in the reader which makes him or her want to continue to read the story. Suspense occurs when the reader does not know what is about to happen and is unsure or uncertain about what will occur.

Some ways to create suspense are listed below:

1. Creating an atmosphere: An atmosphere is a feeling or mood created by the writer using description, setting or dialog. An obvious and overused atmosphere is created in horror movies by using stormy weather, a dark night, a house in the middle of nowhere; this kind of atmosphere is used so often in horror movies that everyone can recognize it. Describing the weather is a very important way to create atmosphere: Bright, sunny days create a happy feeling; dreary weather creates a dismal or gloomy mood.

2. Using foreshadowing: Foreshadowing is a reference to what lies ahead, a hint of what is to occur. A dead mountain goat in a story about mountain climbing could foreshadow an accident on that mountain. A writer who provides these kinds of hints makes the reader want to continue reading.

3. Delaying the climax: The climax is the highest point of tension, the point where the conflict is usually resolved in a story. By inserting events which delay the climax, the writer is able to create suspense or uncertainty in the reader.

4. *Starting in the middle of the action:* We are all used to stories which begin: *Once upon a time there was a little girl named...* We are so accustomed to stories which begin this way that we can lose interest before the action even begins. But starting *the story in the middle of the action can create interest. A story could begin: I lay* there in the abandoned cellar surrounded by what seemed like snakes. The writer can begin in the middle and then go back and fill in details and events to show how the narrator got into this predicament.

By hiding information from the reader or by presenting information to create an atmosphere, the writer can create an interesting story.

3. WRITING A NARRATIVE

EXERCISE 1 ON CREATING SUSPENSE IN A STORY

The following are the opening lines of actual stories by professional writers. For each opening, decide:

1. Is this a good opening or a weak opening?
2. Why?

Write your answers in the space provided after each opening.

When you have complete this assignment on your own, share your ideas with your group. Decide as a group which opening is the most effective, and put a star next to it.

1. "We're going through!" The commander's voice was like thin ice breaking.
        --James Thurber, The Secret Life of Walter Mitty

    _____

    _____

    _____

2. At one time there lived in Lisbon a certain Dom Luiz de Faria who later sailed away in order to see the world, and having visited the greater part of it, died on an island as remote as one's imagination can picture.
        --Karel Capek, The Island

    _____

    _____

    _____

3. I was an untruthful little boy. It was because of my reading: my imagination was always working overtime.
        --Isaac Babel, In the Basement

    _____

    _____

    _____

3. WRITING A NARRATIVE

EXERCISE 2 ON CREATING SUSPENSE IN A STORY

This activity may be completed in pairs with each pair of students working on one topic. Then the topics may be shared by the entire class or groups in the class. The class may vote for the best opening line created by the students.

Choose one of the topics below and write an effective opening sentence for a short story based on that topic.

1. The Worst Thing That Happened To Me Last Summer
2. A Voyage To The Moon
3. Stella the Stegosaurus
4. The Shopping Mall
5. Meeting My Favorite Rock Star
6. The Best Idea I Ever Had
7. The Cave
8. Beans--Nothing But Beans

_____

_____

_____

EXERCISE 3 ON CREATING SUSPENSE IN A STORY

This activity may be completed in pairs with each pair of students working on one topic. Then the topics may be shared by the entire class or groups in the class.

Write the opening paragraph for a short story on any topic you wish. Begin with a strong effective opening by starting in the middle of the action.

Try to capture an effective atmosphere by:

- using weather to create a mood:

  - good weather for a happy experience
  - gloomy weather for an uncertain future
  - stormy weather for horrifying adventure

- foreshadowing future events.

4. WRITING A DESCRIPTION

Description is the art of creating pictures in words--pictures of people, places or objects. The purpose of describing is to let the reader come as close as possible to *seeing* whatever is being described; the author tries to create a mental picture in the reader's imagination. Description is often used as part of narration or exposition. It can, however, also stand alone as a piece of writing.

There are two forms of description:

- **Factual Description** is used in expository writing. The purpose of factual description is objectivity; that is, the writer tries to be an outside observer; he or she does not present his opinions or impressions--only the facts. Factual description is used in want ads in newspapers, in many school textbooks (especially science and geography books), in courts of law, or in police records. It may read like an entry in an encyclopedia or a scientific textbook where the facts are more important than personal impressions. Factual description creates a picture which is more like a diagram or a graph or a chart for the reader to envision what is being described.

- **Literary Description** is used in narrative writing or in poetry. Literary description may be subjective; that is, the writer may convey his or her own impressions of a person or scene while describing it. The writer may also appeal to the reader's imagination by creating images or feelings for the reader. Literary descriptions may be used in telling stories to present a picture of the setting (time and place) or of the characters (both their appearance and their personality). Literary description attempts to create a photograph or a painting for the reader; like a painting (particularly an impressionist painting), it may present suggestions which allow the reader's imagination to come into play.

4. WRITING A DESCRIPTION

AN EXAMPLE OF A FACTUAL DESCRIPTION

What follows is a factual description of the human heart. Note that the author has attempted to be completely objective; there are no personal opinions expressed. The description reads like an entry in an encyclopedia or a textbook.

> The human heart is a muscular organ about the size of a person's fist. It makes up less than one per cent of a human being's body weight. Its function is to receive blood from the veins and transmit the blood through the arteries. The heart is situated behind the lower part of the breastbone, slightly to the left side of the body. It is roughly conical in shape with the base directed upward and to the right. It touches the chest wall between the fifth and sixth ribs.

EXERCISE 1 ON THE FACTUAL DESCRIPTION

1. The factual description makes use of clear and precise adjectives to describe the nouns. There are two precise adjectives used in this passage. List each one in the space below and tell what each one describes.

   _____

   _____

2. Make a list of eight clear and specific nouns used by the writer in this passage.

   _____   _____   _____   _____

   _____   _____   _____   _____

3. Note that the writer does not use personal opinion or judgment in this description. Why would it be wrong for the author to say: "The human heart is the most important organ in the body"?

   _____

   _____

4. WRITING A DESCRIPTION

EXERCISE 2 ON THE FACTUAL DESCRIPTION

What follows is a factual description of a suspect in a crime, but it contains some personal opinions and judgments. It does not stick to the facts.

Cross out the personal opinions and judgments in the description. Change any of them into factual descriptions. Then in small groups, explain why you have crossed out these lines and why you have made the changes.

The man was about six feet tall and looked a little too fat. He had dark hair but not a very fashionable hair style; he looked like someone had put a bowl on his head to cut his hair. He had a scar on his left cheek, extending from his ear to the bridge of his nose. Probably he had been in a fight at one time and that's how he got the scar. He had a tattoo of a rose with a dagger through it on his right forearm, but it wasn't a very good one. He wore dirty, old blue jeans which didn't look like he bought them in a very good shop. He wore a tattered, green and grey sweatshirt with some writing on the front and a picture of a bull's head on the back. He was breathing heavily as if he had asthma or a bad case of allergies. I could tell he was just itching for a fight because he looked so mean and cruel.

4. WRITING A DESCRIPTION

EXERCISE 3 ON THE FACTUAL DESCRIPTION

The writer of a literary description tries to create a character for the reader; that is why a literary description can appeal to a reader's imagination through its use of suggestions and imagery. A factual description, however, tries to show reality, what is rather than what might be.

Write a factual description on one of the following topics. Remember to try to be objective by keeping opinions and judgments out of the description. Use specific nouns and precise verbs, in addition to effective adjectives and adverbs.

- a description of one of your parents

- a description of a close friend

- a description of your bedroom

- a description of an amusement park

- a description of a scene in the city

- a description of a scene in the country

4. WRITING A DESCRIPTION

AN EXAMPLE OF A LITERARY DESCRIPTION

What follows is a literary description of a character named Tom King, a poor, aging boxer in the story <u>A Piece of Steak</u> by Jack London. Note that the author is subjective and uses suggestions to paint the picture in the reader's imagination.

> But it was Tom King's face that advertised him unmistakably for what he was. It was the face of a typical prize-fighter; of one who had put in long years of service in the squared ring and, by that means, developed and emphasized all the marks of the fighting beast. It was distinctly a lowering countenance, and, that no feature of it might escape notice, it was clean-shaven. The lips were shapeless, and constituted a mouth harsh to excess, that was like a gash in his face. The jaw was aggressive, brutal, heavy. The eyes, slow of movement and heavy-lidded, were almost expressionless under the shaggy, indrawn brows. Sheer animal that he was, the eyes were the most animal-like feature about him. The forehead slanted quickly back to the hair, which, clipped close, showed every bump of a villainous-looking head. A nose, twice-broken and moulded variously by countless blows, and a cauliflower ear, permanently swollen and distorted to twice its size, completed his adornment, while the beard, fresh-shaven as it was, sprouted in the skin and gave the face a blue-black stain. All together, it was the face of a man to be afraid of in a dark alley or lonely place.

EXERCISE 1 ON THE LITERARY DESCRIPTION

1. Choose three details which Jack London uses to describe Tom King. What words are especially appropriate in these descriptions?

   _____

   _____

2. Make a list of two subjective phrases which the writer uses in this passage:

   _____

   _____

4. WRITING A DESCRIPTION

TECHNIQUES OF LITERARY DESCRIPTION

The literary description, like the factual description, uses the following techniques to create a vivid picture:

1. specific detail
2. precise nouns and verbs
3. well chosen adjectives and adverbs.

Unlike the factual description, the literary description also tries to use words and phrases for their suggested meanings in order to appeal to the reader's imagination. The following techniques may be used to appeal to the reader's senses:

1. imagery
2. words which suggest sound.

EXERCISE 2 ON THE LITERARY DESCRIPTION

List **ten** specific details which you could use to describe any three of the following:

- your house

- an old woman whom you know

- a ride at an amusement park

- the way you would like to look if you could

- a famous building (such as the CN Tower or the White House)

- a football, baseball or hockey coach

- your favorite toy when you were younger

- a pet.

4. WRITING A DESCRIPTION

TECHNIQUES OF LITERARY DESCRIPTION

EXERCISE 3 ON THE LITERARY DESCRIPTION

A writer who chooses specific rather than general words will communicate most effectively. Writers should examine the nouns and verbs which they use in writing to see if more specific words can be used. A sentence like *The man walked into the room* does communicate an idea, but it is a very general one. *The drunk stumbled into the salon* uses *two specific nouns and a specific verb to communicate a much clearer picture. The waiter waltzed into the kitchen* offers another clear picture. Note that the latter two examples essentially say *The man walked into the room*, but they also say much more.

Choose precise nouns to replace **man** and **room** and specific verbs to replace **walked** in the sentence *The man walked into the room*. Write them in the corresponding place in the chart.

The man	walked	into the room
1.		
2.		
3.		
4.		
5.		
6.		
7.		

4. WRITING A DESCRIPTION

TECHNIQUES OF LITERARY DESCRIPTION

EXERCISE 4 ON THE LITERARY DESCRIPTION

Adjectives and adverbs can be very helpful in writing description, but the writer must recognize that they are not the only way to describe something. A piece of descriptive writing made up only of adjectives and adverbs would be quite dull.

An **adjective** is a word which describes a **noun**. In the phrase *blue socks*, the word *blue* is an adjective which describes the noun *socks*.

Although it can describe (or modify) other words, an **adverb** generally describes the action of a **verb**. It answers one of the following questions to a verb: when? where? why? how? how much? In the sentence *The boy talked slowly*, the adverb *slowly* tells *how* the boy talked.

In the following charts, write four adjectives and adverbs which describe each of the following nouns: Try to choose colorful, descriptive adjectives.

Noun	Adjective 1	Adjective 2	Adjective 3	Adjective 4
teacher				
city				
beach				
bird				

Noun	Adverb 1	Adverb 2	Adverb 3	Adverb 4
sang				
sat				
acted				
played				

4. WRITING A DESCRIPTION

TECHNIQUES OF LITERARY DESCRIPTION

IMAGERY

Another technique, called **imagery**, can help a writer to describe what he or she wants to say. An image is a picture created in words.

A writer often creates an image by using comparison, by saying that one thing is **like** something totally different. If the writer states this comparison directly, using the words *like* or *as*, the image is called a **simile**. *Graham has a head like a rock* is an example of a simile: Graham's head and a rock are two different things, but they share common characteristics, such as *hardness*. Using a simile from time to time can help a writer to create a clear picture for the reader. The writer should, however, not use similes that are heard every day; instead, he or she should try to create original similes. Some common similes which should be **avoided** are:

- cool as a cucumber
- cold as ice
- My love is like a red rose.

A **metaphor** is an indirect comparison. Whereas a simile says one thing is *like* another, a metaphor says that one thing is another. *Graham has a rock for a head* is a metaphor which implies that Graham's head and a rock have similar qualities. Again, the effective writer should create original metaphors instead of using ones that are often heard or seen in print. Some metaphors to **avoid** are:

- birds of a feather
- elbow grease
- dead as a doornail
- clear as mud

A third type of comparison is **personification**. Personification is giving human qualities to something which is not human. *The sun smiled on the survivors of the shipwreck* is an example of personification: The sun, an inanimate object, is given the human ability to smile. Personification is another technique that can be used sparingly in descriptive writing. *The wind blew* is a dull way to say something; *the wind shrieked and howled* creates a vivid picture for the reader.

4. WRITING A DESCRIPTION

TECHNIQUES OF LITERARY DESCRIPTION

EXERCISES 1 to 3 ON IMAGERY

1. Complete the following chart using original similes. Remember that a simile compares two unlike things using *like or as*.

   a) Love is like... _____

   _____

   b) Olives taste like... _____

   _____

   c) A baby has fingers like... _____

   _____

   d) A winter storm is like... _____

   _____

   e) Gym socks smell like... _____

   _____

2. Complete the following chart using original metaphors. Remember that a metaphor compares two unlike things by saying the on *is* another.

   a) Love is... _____

   _____

   b) Olives are... _____

   _____

   c) A baby has fingers made of ... _____

   _____

   d) A winter storm is... _____

   e) Gym socks are... _____

   _____

3. Now try your hand at personification. Complete the following chart by giving human qualities to the inanimate objects named. Be sure to make each example into a complete sentence.

   a) Love... _____

   _____

   b) Olives... _____

   _____

   c) One January morning... _____

   _____

   d) A winter storm... _____

   _____

   e) Gym socks... _____

   _____

4. Writing Description

TECHNIQUES OF LITERARY DESCRIPTION

EXERCISE 4 ON IMAGERY

In the chart which follows, identify the figure of speech as simile, metaphor or personification in Column A. In Column B, say if you feel this is a good image or a poor one. In Column C, give reasons for you choice in Column B.

Example	A. Identify	B. Good or Poor	C. Reasons
Her voice is soft as honey dripping from a comb.			
A new idea jumped into his head just when he needed it.			
My little brother was as good as gold at the concert.			
Cairo, the capital of Egypt, is the Jewel of the Nile.			
My baseball cap is like a comfortable old friend.			

4. WRITING A DESCRIPTION

TECHNIQUES OF LITERARY DESCRIPTION

SOUND

Words were created first so people could speak and words have distinct sounds. Sometimes words are like music; often they are like noise. A good writer will use the sounds of words to their advantage.

Alliteration is the repetition of the sounds of consonants in words. *Peter Piper picked a peck of pickled peppers* is not only a tongue-twister but also an example of alliteration. In poetry, alliteration can sometimes be a useful device, whereas in other writing it may be cute-sounding but is not always effective.

A more effective device is **onomatopoeia**, pronounced ON-OH-MOT-OH-PEE-YA. Onomatopoeia means that the sound of the words imitates what the words mean. John Keats wrote: *The murmurous haunts of flies on summer eves*. The repetition of the *s* and *z* sounds do imitate the sound made by the flies.

Some examples of onomatopoeia, words whose sounds imitate their meanings, are:

- the buzz of the bees
- the tick-tock of the clock
- whippoorwill
- the hoot owl
- splash
- clatter
- clang
- pop

The sound of words is controlled by the consonants in the words: The **s** sound hisses; **t**, **c**, **k** and the hard **g** are sharp sounds; **m** and **n** are soft sounds.

4. WRITING A DESCRIPTION

TECHNIQUES OF LITERARY DESCRIPTION

EXERCISE ON SOUND

Following are some words with distinctive sounds. Use each word in a sentence which reveals its unique sound. Try also to create an image to match the sound.

1. *murky*: _____

_____

_____

2. *squeak*: _____

_____

_____

3. *belch*: _____

_____

_____

4. *squish*: _____

_____

_____

5. *gurgle*: _____

_____

_____

5. USING THE WRITING PROCESS

The writing process is not new to schools in North America. Today, students learn to use the writing process as soon as they begin to learn to write. Much of what is said here, then, will be nothing new to teachers of writing. However, perhaps isolating the procedure on the next few pages will help teachers to teach and students to learn.

The writing process consists of four major steps:

- prewriting
- editing and revising
- writing the first draft
- writing the final copy

Steps 2 and 3 may be repeated as many times as necessary; the student may write, edit and revise successive drafts until he or she is satisfied with the work. D.H. Lawrence, the distinguished novelist, wrote seven drafts of his masterpiece, <u>Sons and Lovers</u>, and was still not completely satisfied.

PREWRITING

It is very difficult to sit down and write effectively without doing any preplanning. Many educators consider the first stage of the writing process to be the most important.

Prewriting consists of four parts:

- Brainstorming
- Selection of ideas to be used
- Research
- Prewriting plan

1. BRAINSTORMING:

The first stage of the writing process, after choosing the topic, is the brainstorming stage. The purpose of this stage is to use what the student already knows to begin to compile information which will be used for the final draft.

At the brainstorming stage, the student writes down on a piece of paper any information which pertains to the topic as these ideas come into his or her mind. The student may use mind-mapping techniques if these are easier.

The next four pages show sheets which may be used for brainstorming each of the three types of compositions in this resource:

- the exposition
- the narrative
- description

Teachers may use these sheets or devise their own. It is important, however, that students be given some guidance to teach them techniques for brainstorming. The teacher should not assume that students already know how to do this.

5. USING THE WRITING PROCESS

PREWRITING

BRAINSTORMING AN EXPOSITION

TOPIC: What do you intend to explain?

_____

_____

Fill in the chart with as much information as you know:

Who is involved?	What is involved?
Where did it take place?	**When did it take place?**
How did it happen?	**What events occurred?**

5. USING THE WRITING PROCESS

PREWRITING

BRAINSTORMING A NARRATIVE (Part 1)

Fill in the chart with your first ideas.

List five possible settings for a story (time and place):

1.

2.

3.

4.

5.

Briefly describe five possible characters who interest you (name and short description):

1.

2.

3.

4.

5.

List five possible events which could occur to one or more of these characters in one or more of the settings you have listed:

1.

2.

3.

4.

5.

5. USING THE WRITING PROCESS

PREWRITING

BRAINSTORMING A NARRATIVE (Part 2)

Fill in the chart with ideas chosen from completing part 1.

List the setting you will use for your story (time and place):

Describe the setting:

Choose the central character for your story. State his or her name and provide a short description of the character's appearance and personality:

List other characters you may use:

Choose an event which will occur. List the sequence of events which will take place:

5. USING THE WRITING PROCESS

PREWRITING

BRAINSTORMING A DESCRIPTION

TOPIC: What or whom do you intend to describe?

_____

_____

In the center of this page, do a mind-map, starting with what the person, place or object that you intend to describe looks like. If you are describing a person, add a section on the personality.

5. USING THE WRITING PROCESS

PREWRITING

2. RESEARCH:

Research may not be required in the types of student writing presented in this resource. Certain assignments may only require brainstorming.

However, research may be required for any of the following reasons:

- The student is writing an exposition on a topic unknown to him or her, a topic which is not considered common knowledge, such as *The Wright Brothers* or a country which he or she has never visited.

- The student is writing a short story set in a particular place or time and needs to know more about that place or time.

- The student is writing a factual description about someone or something with which he or she is not familiar.

Teachers often assume that students know how to research. Quite often, students simply copy information from an encyclopedia. They need to be taught how to do research well. The teacher should stress the following techniques:

- Students should read the encyclopedia, textbook or whatever source and then try to express the ideas in their own words. This will check to see that students are really understanding what they have read.

- Students should prepare a list of relevant questions (or the teacher may provide such a list). The kinds of questions asked in the brainstorming sheets on pages 46 and 47 of this resource could be helpful. Alternatively, students could ask simple questions such as: *Who? When? Where? How? Why?*

- Students should be cautioned not to write down every word they read. As they put the ideas into their own words, they should also select the information that seems to be important and only write that down.

- Students should note the source of all information they are writing down. Particularly in the higher grades, students will need to provide these sources with their finished writing.

5. USING THE WRITING PROCESS

PREWRITING

3. SELECTION OF IDEAS TO BE USED:

After completing several pages of brainstorming and research, the student should have many ideas for the composition. Now is the time to start selecting the ideas which will actually be used and to organize them in some logical form.

Perhaps the easiest way for students to do this is to follow this pattern:

1. Group the ideas that are similar. Each grouping will eventually form one paragraph in the composition.

2. Give a title to each group. In a description of a person, for example, the titles may simply be: *Personality* and *Appearance*.

3. If any groups seem to be very long, they should be subdivided into several related *groupings. Appearance*, for example, might be subdivided into *Clothing, Body and* Stature, Face, etc.

4. The subdividing of groups in step 3 may lead to a new organization. *Personality*, for example, may become part of the other groupings, as it is revealed by the persons clothing, body shape, face.

It may take several attempts (and several pages) to do this grouping and regrouping. However, the results will be worth it.

4. PREWRITING PLAN:

The prewriting Plan may be the most important step in writing a composition. If it is done well, the prewriting plan shows the entire composition on one sheet of paper. (Students should use larger sheets of paper for long or more complicated pieces of writing, but shorter pieces should fit on one $8\frac{1}{2}$" by 11" sheet.)

An example of a prewriting plan is shown on the next page.

5. USING THE WRITING PROCESS

PREWRITING

4. PREWRITING PLAN:

A typical **Prewriting Plan** will look something like the following:

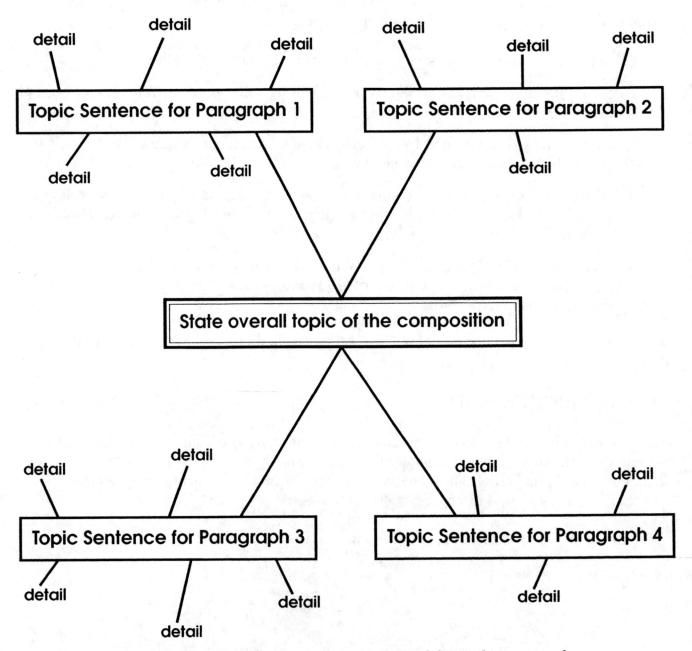

The writer will supply as many details as are required for each paragraph.

5. USING THE WRITING PROCESS

WRITING THE FIRST DRAFT

Most beginning writers need to work on content and organization; style will come later; and mechanics can be helped by proofreading, editing or using one of many computer programs. The steps in the Prewriting stage will help to provide adequate content for the essay. What follows is a simple pattern which should help the student to organize the composition. The pattern can be changed to meet the requirements of the specific writing task.

1. THE OPENING PARAGRAPH:

• **Step 1:** Begin with a sentence which catches the reader's interest. In a narrative this may mean starting in the middle of the action. In a description or exposition, the opening may be a quotation or an interesting idea related to the topic. The idea of the opening sentence may be developed or explained in several sentences which follow it.

• **Step 2:** In a story, develop the paragraph as necessary; be sure to include necessary background information in the first few paragraphs. In an exposition or description, state the overall topic in a single sentence. Do not explain the topic at this point unless it is absolutely necessary to do so. The topic can be explained as it is developed later in the composition.

• **Step 3:** Conclude the paragraph by restating the topic. Ignore this step when writing a narrative.

Various patterns can be developed for beginning each form of writing. The requirements of a particular piece of writing will determine the pattern to be used. It is important that the writer catch the interest of the reader at the beginning of the piece; it is also important in an exposition or a description to provide some kind of overview as a guide for the reader. A sample opening paragraph for an exposition follows on page 55.

5. USING THE WRITING PROCESS

WRITING THE FIRST DRAFT

2. A SAMPLE OPENING PARAGRAPH:

What follows is an opening paragraph for an exposition based on the topic, *The Wright* Brothers.

Statement to catch the reader's interest	From the time when human beings first saw birds in the sky, men and women have dreamed of one day experiencing the
Statement of topic	freedom of flight. Wilbur and Orville Wright shared that same dream. From their early
Ideas which will be discussed in the composition	days growing up in Dayton, Ohio, through the years of invention in their bicycle shop, to their experiments in Kitty Hawk, they longed to reach for the skies. Their dreams became
Concluding statement	a reality with a twelve second flight on December 17, 1903.

Note that the writer of this paragraph has a clear idea of what he or she will be discussing in the body of the exposition--and so does the reader.

5. USING THE WRITING PROCESS

WRITING THE FIRST DRAFT

3. PARAGRAPHS IN THE BODY OF THE COMPOSITION:

Paragraphs in the body of the composition follow a pattern to maintain unity and coherence. Unity and coherence are discussed in detail on pages 4 of this resource.

A typical paragraph for an exposition or description will follow these steps:

- **Step 1:** Starting with a transition if necessary, write the topic sentence.

- **Step 2:** Explain the topic sentence as necessary. The topic sentence may be self-explanatory and may need no further explanation. On the other hand, the topic sentence may require one or several sentences for explanation.

- **Step 3:** Provide the details which develop the idea of the topic sentence and give any necessary explanations.

- **Step 4:** Sum up the paragraph and refer to the topic sentence if necessary.

This pattern will be followed for each paragraph in the composition. Students need to remember that each paragraph develops one of the major ideas in the composition. Thus, a composition with three major ideas will be five paragraphs in length--an introductory paragraph, one paragraph for each of the three ideas and a concluding paragraph. A composition with four major ideas will be six paragraphs in length, and so on.

A **short story** or **narrative** will follow a somewhat different paragraph structure. There will perhaps be less explanation and more action, but a new action requires a new paragraph. In addition, when **dialog** is used, it is common practice to change paragraph when the writer changes speaker. This allows the reader to stay on track without the constant repetition of *he said* or *she said*.

5. USING THE WRITING PROCESS

WRITING THE FIRST DRAFT

4. THE CONCLUDING PARAGRAPH:

The normal function of a concluding paragraph is to sum up what has been said in the composition. This is certainly true in an exposition or description, but is less obvious in a narrative.

- **Concluding an Exposition:**

Usually the concluding paragraph sums up by rephrasing the major explanations which have been presented or by making a recommendation or a comment based on the explanations. Often the concluding paragraph is very short, perhaps only a sentence or two. A concluding paragraph on *The Wright Brothers* might read:

- *Although the plane only flew for twelve seconds, Orville and Wilbur Wright knew that they had accomplished something no one had been able to do before. They were true pioneers of flight.*

- **Concluding a Description:**

Again the concluding paragraph may sum up the major idea of a description in a sentence or two. A conclusion for a description of a person named *Bob* may conclude:

- *Bob's sense of humor and honesty endeared him to all who knew him. He was a truly good human being.*

- **Concluding a Narrative:**

Usually order is restored at the end of a story; it may be--and probably is--a different order than at the beginning of the story. Usually stories end in some sort of hope, even if the ending is unhappy. Some stories leave the reader hanging; The Lady Or The Tiger?, for example, leaves the conclusion to the reader to decide. Readers *often do not like to be left hanging. Avoid a conclusion such as: And then I woke* up. The dream ending is considered old-hat.

5. USING THE WRITING PROCESS

EDITING AND REVISING

Editing and revising are not merely proofreading. Rather they comprise a very important step in the writing process at which stage the student will do a thorough evaluation of his or her writing and will receive feedback from peers or parents. Students need to be taught **how** to edit; they should not simply be expected to know how to do it. Unless students are taught how to edit, peer edits will consist of comments like "Good work" or "Check spelling"--and these comments are of little practical use in improving a piece of writing.

Students should begin to learn how to edit in the later grades of elementary school, and continue to learn how to edit through secondary school. The editing directions which follow are designed for elementary school and early secondary school students. More complete editing suggestions will be found in *How to Write an Essay*, SSR1-08.

Students often have more difficulty editing their own work than editing someone else's work. It is, therefore, good practice for students to peer edit, not only to help the other student to improve, but also to learn how to improve their own writing.

Editing works best if the student keeps in mind the four categories--Content, Organization, Style and **Mechanics**. Each of these categories will be examined briefly in the following pages. There are various activities, particularly in the Mechanics section, which will help students learn how to edit their own and their classmates' work.

Peer editing should be looked at in two ways: A good peer edit not only helps the writer, but also the editor. Students perhaps learn more from editing someone else's writing than from editing their own. Perhaps this knowledge gained from editing other students' work will eventually carry over to their own writing.

5. USING THE WRITING PROCESS

EDITING AND REVISING - EDITING FOR CONTENT

The teacher should always make perfectly clear to students what the expectations of an assignment are. These expectations will normally highlight what is expected in terms of content. Teachers should provide students with a clear editing sheet for any particular assignment, if the teacher expects students to edit their own or each other's work for content.

Bearing that in mind, the teacher may use what follows as part of the editing sheet for a composition.

Editing an Exposition or a Description:

1. Have all the relevant questions been answered in the piece of writing. Relevant questions may include:

   • Who? • What? • Where? • When? • Why? • How?

2. Has sufficient detail been provided by the writer? If so, provide examples of good detail. If not, where in the composition could more detail be added? Do you have any suggestions that may add detail to the composition?

3. Are there parts of the composition which you do not understand? Is this lack of understanding caused by the way the composition is written or by the omission of important information? If important information is missing where could it be added?

4. Is the composition interesting? Does it have an interesting opening and an interesting conclusion? Are the body paragraphs interesting? If so, which ones? If not, which ones?

Editing a Narrative:

1. **Opening:**
   • Does the story open in an interesting way?
   • Are there better ways to begin the story? If yes, what are they?

2. **Plot:**
   • Does the plot move at an appropriate pace?
   • Does it reach a climax?
   • Is there a satisfying conclusion to the plot?

3. **Setting:**
   • Has the writer provided enough detail about time and place so that the reader gets a "feel" for the setting?
   • Is the setting described in a paragraph by itself? If yes, does this work? If no, should it be described separately or has the writer done a good job of describing it indirectly?

4. **Characterization:**
   • Do the characters exhibit real emotions and behavior?
   • Are the characters only names without personality or appearance? If yes, where might the writer describe or develop the characters in the story? What character traits might be appropriate?

5. **Theme:**
   • What is the story about?
   • Does the message come through clearly? If yes, where does this occur? If no, what could the writer do to make a clearer message?

Sections 3 and 4 on *Editing an Exposition or a Description* could also be used here.

5. USING THE WRITING PROCESS

EDITING AND REVISING

EDITING FOR ORGANIZATION

Editing an Exposition or a Description:

1. **Opening Paragraph:**

   - Does the opening paragraph catch the reader's interest? Why or why not?

   - Does the reader have a sense of what the composition will be about after reading the opening paragraph? Should more detail be added to the opening paragraph? Is the opening paragraph too detailed?

   - Are transitions used to provide coherence?

   - Is there a concluding sentence?

2. **Paragraphs in the Body:**

   - Does each paragraph begin with a topic sentence?

   - Is each paragraph unified; that is, does each paragraph discuss only one main idea?

   - Are transitions used to provide coherence within each paragraph and between paragraphs?

   - Is there a concluding sentence for each paragraph?

3. **Conclusion:**

   - Does the conclusion sum up the main ideas of the composition?

   - Is the conclusion too brief?

   - Is the conclusion interesting?

Additional Editing for a Narrative:

Use any relevant questions listed above, but ask the following question:

   - Has the writer changed paragraph each time there is a new speaker?

5. USING THE WRITING PROCESS

EDITING AND REVISING - EDITING FOR STYLE

Style is the most sophisticated of the four components of the writing process and is developed through writing programs to and including the university level. Students at elementary school can begin their study of style through writing and editing.

We often use the word *style* in reference to fashion, as in *style of clothes*. A person with **style is said to possess a knowledge of the latest trends, a certain flair. In writing, style** refers to the way the writer uses **languages** to create specific **effects** or to reach certain **goals**.

Thus, **style is the use of words and the arrangement of words to form sentences.**

Some preliminary work has already been done on style. Please see pages 36 to 43 of this resource.

Questions to Ask about Style:

1. Does the writer use effective and precise nouns and verbs in the composition? Which are particularly good examples? Which nouns and verbs are particularly vague or colorless?

2. Are adjectives and adverbs used effectively? Are they overused? Might some of them be replaced with more colorful nouns and verbs?

3. Does the writer use imagery? Is the imagery effective? Does the writer use old and worn out similes and metaphors? Does the writer create new and original similes and metaphors?

4. Does the writer use the sounds of words effectively? Do the sounds of words present an appropriate tone?

5. USING THE WRITING PROCESS

EDITING AND REVISING

EDITING FOR MECHANICS

Mechanics in writing refers to some of the most basic components of language programs in the elementary school--spelling, grammar, punctuation, and sentence structure.

Not all students have the same problems with mechanics. Some are good spellers; others are not. Some have persistent problems with certain aspects of grammar; others have a good grammar sense. Some students speak and write in sentences; others always speak and write in incomplete or run-on sentences. While the school curriculum provides basic instruction in all these aspects of mechanics, some students will need constant reminders of the areas they can improve.

There are many aids available for students who have weaknesses in mechanics. Spell-Check on computers is a valuable aid, but requires a knowledgeable proof-reader. Grammar checks on computers are more difficult to use, since much of the way we write depends on personal preference.

Although there are many individual differences, generally students seem to have difficulty with only a few areas of mechanics. Those which students often need to focus on are:

- common errors in spelling
- the use of the apostrophe
- the use of a consistent verb tense
- agreement of pronouns and antecedents
- the use of the semicolon

Only the first two (common errors in spelling and use of the apostrophe) are dealt with in this resource. Teachers and students needing information on the other topics should consult *How to Write an Essay*, SSR1-08.

5. USING THE WRITING PROCESS

EDITING AND REVISING

EDITING FOR MECHANICS

Common Errors in Spelling:

Many students have no difficulty in spelling and are able to see their errors clearly when they edit their writing. Others have a great deal of difficulty. There are, however, words which students consistently misspell and students need to be aware of these. A writer can easily improve spelling if he or she is on the lookout for specific words which cause problems. Following is a list of words that appear incorrectly spelled in many students' writing:

- **receive**: The "*I before e*" rule has too many exceptions to be considered a rule. Generally, "*ei*" will follow the letter "*c*" and students need to bear this in mind when writing words like **receive, deceive, conceive, ceiling.**

- **achieve**: There are many words which follow the rule such as: **achieve, friend,** piece, chief and **relieve.**

- **separate**: Note the letter "*a*" follows the "*p*".

- **definite**: Note "*ite*", not "*ate*".

- **their, they're, there**: **Their** is possessive, meaning "belongs to them". **They're** is the contraction for "there are". **There** means "in that place".

- **occurred, occurring, referred, referring, preferred, preferring**: These words double the letter "*r*" before adding "*ed*" and "*ing*". Note also **occurrence** doubles the "*r*", but **reference** and **preference** do not.

- **dependent, independent**: These adjectives are spelled "*ent*". **Dependant** with an "*a*" is a noun often seen on income tax forms to mean "someone who is dependent".

- **words beginning with a prefix such as "un", "re" or "mis"**: Simply add the prefix to the word, as in **unnecessary, recommend** or **misspell.**

Activity on Spelling:

Create your own spelling collage, using a piece of bristol board. Make a list of words you misspell. When a word appears on the list three times, put it on the bristol board collage.

5. USING THE WRITING PROCESS

EDITING AND REVISING

EDITING FOR MECHANICS

The Use of the Apostrophe:

Some students have difficulty using the apostrophe correctly. The rules which follow are very simple. Many writers try to complicate these rules by making exceptions to them, but these rules can cover every major example of the apostrophe.

Uses of the Apostrophe:

- Possession in Nouns
- Contractions

The apostrophe is used to show **possession** or **ownership**. Originally possession was shown in Anglo-Saxon by the addition of the letters "*es*" to a noun. The "*e*" was later omitted and the apostrophe was used in its place.

The apostrophe is also used to show the omission of letters in **contractions**. Contractions are *two words shortened into one word by omitting letters. Some common contractions are didn't* (the letter "o" is omitted), *who's* (meaning who is), *they're* (meaning they are).

Using the Apostrophe for Form Possession:

Singular nouns form possession by adding 's to the noun. Follow this rule and you will always be correct, even if the noun ends in s. Some examples:

- boy = singular noun   boy's = belong to the boy
- Mr. Smith = singular noun   Mr. Smith's = belonging to Mr. Smith
- Brutus = singular noun   Brutus's = belonging to Brutus
- Dickens = singular noun   Dickens's = belonging to Dickens

Plural nouns ending in *s* form possession by adding ' to the noun. Example:

- boys = plural noun   boys' = belonging to the boys

Plural nouns not ending in *s* form possession by adding 's to the noun. Some examples:

- children = plural noun   children's = belonging to the children
- data = plural noun   data's = belonging to the data
- women = plural noun   women's = belonging to the women

5. USING THE WRITING PROCESS

EDITING AND REVISING

EDITING FOR MECHANICS

The Use of the Apostrophe (Continued):

Writers who follow the rules on page 61 will **never be wrong** in forming possession. There are writers and grammarians who complicate these rules by saying that if the *singular noun ending in s* is pronounced *es* then one adds *'s*; if the word is not pronounced *es* then add only the apostrophe; *Jesus' sake* (meaning for the sake of Jesus) would then be pronounced *Jesus sake*, but *Jesus's sake* would be pronounced *Jesuses sake*. This kind of usage is often found in hymns or prayers using poetry, but for most practical purposes it unnecessarily complicates a simple rule of the English language (and really there are not very many simple rules that apply, are there? So why complicate it?)

Using the Apostrophe with Pronouns:

The apostrophe is never used with personal pronouns to form possession; it is only to form contractions. Here are some examples:

- *who's* = who is; the possessive is *whose*
- *their's* does not exist; the possessive is *theirs*
- *our's* similarly does not exist; the possessive is *ours*

Indefinite pronouns, however, use the apostrophe to form possession. Indefinite pronouns are words like *one, everyone, anyone*, etc. Here are some examples:

- everyone's job
- one's own work

These simple rules will govern the use of the apostrophe. Many students have difficulty with the concept because they either confuse the meaning of the term possession or they are overwhelmed by the number of seeming exceptions. If the teacher stresses that there are not exceptions, then the task becomes easier for students to learn.

5. USING THE WRITING PROCESS

EDITING AND REVISING

EDITING FOR MECHANICS

The Use of the Apostrophe (Continued):

Activity on the Use of the Apostrophe:

1. Form the possessive of each of the following words:

    a) John   _____
    b) athlete   _____
    c) John Keats   _____
    d) United States   _____
    e) United States of America   _____
    f) India   _____
    g) potatoes   _____
    h) Donovan Bailey   _____
    i) sisters   _____
    j) Mississippi   _____

2. Four words in the following sentences contain incorrect apostrophes. Four other words are missing required apostrophes. In groups of two or three, decide which are the four incorrect words and which four words need apostrophes. Be prepared to support you answers.

> In his works Dicken's often writes about the evils of society. He knows about debtors prison because his father spent some time in a prison. He knows also about the evils' of the workhouse, where people who are very poor have to live in order to eat. Oliver Twist is a character who's life begins in a workhouse, but Oliver is adopted by a rich family. However, Dickens does not believe that life is easy. Oliver is kidnapped by Fagin and his boys who are pickpockets. The boys steal from people but they arent sorry for it. The pickpockets' job is really to support Fagins lifestyle by providing him with articles he may sell. An acquaintance of Fagin named Nancy tells Olivers new parents where they can find him, but Nancy's boyfriend, Bill Sykes, kills' her. Finally, Fagin and Bill Sykes are punished for their crimes. Dickens novel, <u>Oliver Twist</u>, clearly shows problems in society.

5. USING THE WRITING PROCESS

WRITING THE FINAL COPY

If a student has followed all the steps in this resource, writing the final copy of the composition will be simple, because all the work has been done. A student who wrote the first draft on a word-processor has been able to make revisions quite simply. Now all that needs to be done is to put the program through spell-check and format it to fit pages.

What follows is a check-list for the final copy of the composition:

- Be sure that the composition is double-spaced and that adequate margins have been left on all sides.

- Use the accepted format for footnotes and bibliography if these are required. See *How to Write an Essay*, SSR1-08, for additional information.

- Add a title page. Some teacher like students to put their compositions into duotangs because these add a touch of formality to the assignment; other teachers do not like duotangs because they add more bulk. Since the teacher has to carry the essays home or to another room to begin the arduous job of marking, he or she may resent the added bulk caused by duotangs. The student should check with the teacher before submitting the composition.

- Proofread the composition carefully. Even a good spell-check program will not be able to catch typographical errors.